Church Year

Series A
Pentecost II

Leaders Guide

By Kenneth Wagener
Edited by Thomas J. Doyle

CPH
SAINT LOUIS

Write to the Library for the Blind, 1333 S. Kirkwood Road, St. Louis, MO 63122-7295 to obtain this study in braille or large print for the visually impaired.

Quotations from *Luther's Works* are from the American edition: vol. 21, copyright © 1956, and vol. 23, copyright © 1959, by Concordia Publishing House. All rights reserved.

Some quotations are from *What Luther Says,* compiled by Ewald M. Plass. Copyright © 1959 by Concordia Publishing House. All rights reserved.

Scripture taken from the HOLY BIBLE: NEW INTERNATIONAL VERSION®. NIV®. Copyright © 1973, 1978, 1984 by International Bible Society. Used by permission of Zondervan Publishing House. All rights reserved.

Copyright © 1996 Concordia Publishing House
3558 South Jefferson Avenue, St. Louis, MO 63118-3968
Manufactured in the United States of America

Contents

Introduction

About the Series

This course is 1 of 12 in the Church Year series. The Bible studies in this series are tied to the 3-year lectionary. These studies give participants the opportunity to explore the Old Testament lesson (or lesson from the book of Acts during the Easter season), the Epistle lesson, and the Gospel lesson appointed for each Sunday of the church year. Also, optional studies give participants the opportunity to study in-depth the lessons appointed for festivals during the church year that fall on days other than Sunday (e.g., Ascension, Reformation, Christmas Eve, Christmas Day, Epiphany, Maundy Thursday, Good Friday).

Book 1 for years A, B, and C in the lectionary series will include 17 studies for the Scripture lessons appointed for the Sundays and festival days in Advent, Christmas, and Epiphany. Book 2 will include 17 studies for the lessons appointed for the Sundays and festival days in Lent and Easter and of lessons appointed for Ascension and Pentecost. Book 3 (15 sessions) and 4 (15 sessions) for years A, B, and C will include studies that focus on the lessons appointed for the Pentecost season.

After a brief review and textual study of the Scripture lessons appointed for a Sunday or festival day, each study is designed to help participants draw conclusions about each of the lessons, compare the lessons, discover a unifying theme in the lessons (if possible), and apply the theme to their lives. At the end of each study, the Scripture lessons for the next Sunday or festival day are assigned for participants to read in preparation for the next study. The Leaders Guide for each course provides additional information on appointed lessons, answers to the questions in the Study Guide, a suggested process for teaching the study, and devotional or worship activities tied to the theme.

May the Holy Spirit richly bless you as you study God's Word!

Session 1

Sixteenth Sunday after Pentecost

Ezekiel 33:7–9; Romans 13:1–10; Matthew 18:15–20

Focus

Theme: *Awesome Authority*

Law/Gospel Focus

Read aloud the Law/Gospel focus.

Objectives

Invite volunteers to read aloud the lesson objectives.

Opening Worship

Lead the group using the responsive prayer provided.

Introduction

Read the introductory paragraphs to the group. Invite general comments or examples to illustrate what you have read. Use the introduction to spark a discussion on the general theme of lack of respect for authority in contemporary society. Move through the items in this section quickly without allowing the discussion to drag.

1. Accept participants' comments. Someone may comment on the erosion of respect for the office of the pastor corresponding to the frequency of news reports that allege abuse by a pastor and a general disrespect for pastoral office often evidenced in popular media. Others may comment on the reluctance of congregations to excommunicate members for fear of possible legal retaliation.
2. Answers will vary. Possibilities include the breakdown of the family, and influence of media, and the prevalent "what's in it for me" attitude among people today.
3. Accept participant responses.

4. Like all traditional institutions, organized religion and religious institutions seem to be a target for unwarranted criticism and contempt. Interestingly enough, society seems to be showing a renewed interest in spirituality. Unfortunately, much of this interest seems directed toward "me focused" New Age type religions.

Inform

If participants have not read the Scripture lessons before class, read each in turn as it is discussed.

1. Most will probably think of a watchman in terms of the guard or sentry whose mission it is to protect those for whom he or she have been given responsibility. The dangers associated with this position include those posed by forces intent upon harming or carrying off those for whom the watchman is responsible. Ezekiel alludes to the threat God gives to the watchman whom He holds accountable to fulfill faithfully the mission of warning those who refuse to turn from their sin.

2. In ancient Israel the watchman's duty was to stand guard against the possible advance of an invading army. If such an advance was to occur, the watchman was to blow the trumpet in warning so the people could take to the sword in their defense. Ezekiel points out that if the watchman sounded the trumpet but the people ignored it and did not take up the sword in their own defense, the watchman was not responsible for their deaths since the people had been warned. The watchman, however, would be held accountable if he saw the coming danger and did not issue the warning. Modern equivalents to the watchmen of old would include the sophisticated missile detection devices that protect the modern nations of the world; sirens, radios, and televisions that warn against an advancing storm; and, of course, friends, pastors, teachers, and others in authority who warn us of possible dangers and their consequences.

3. We can be God's watchmen when we through word and example evidence His power and presence in our lives and as we labor to bring others under the influence of His loving protection and care. We also serve as watchmen for our brothers and sisters in Christ when we encourage and support them in their joys and challenges of their lives and when we at times warn them about consequences of the sin they have allowed to take root in their lives.

4. Paul calls God's people to respect and submit to authorities—even those secular in nature such as the Roman Empire or the political authorities to which we relate in our modern world. Paul reminds us that authorities have been established by God and it is our duty to obey those in authority as evidence that we belong to Him. The two reasons for obeying those in authority are not only because of possible punishment but also because of conscience (v. 5).

5. Paul said, "submit to one another out of reverence for Christ" (Eph. 5:21). As a grateful response to God for all that He has done for us through Christ Jesus, God would have us respectfully oblige ourselves toward all others, valuing all others as those for whom Christ has also died and desires to welcome into His kingdom of believers.

6. If we were capable of obeying the Ten Commandments perfectly, we would live in a world of complete peace and happiness and in total love and respect for one another. Unfortunately, because of sin we are unable to love, obey, and otherwise properly regard God and others. But, thank God, Jesus took our place. He lived the Law perfectly for us and died to pay the penalty our sins deserved.

7. The parable of the 100 sheep illustrate the important motivation for church discipline—to call unrepentant sinners to leave their sins and receive the full and complete forgiveness Christ has provided so that a complete reconciliation may take place.

Connect

Read the introductory section aloud. Underscore the Word of God as the ultimate authority for what Christians believe, profess, and do. Continue with a discussion of the questions.

1. Encourage participants in their responses. Affirm especially those who refer to the power, encouragement, and direction God provides them through His Word as they read and study it on a regular basis. Underscore the unity and strength it provides those who study it regularly together as a group.

2. Answers will vary. In the words of the Great Commission, our Lord reminded His followers that He possesses all authority in heaven and on earth as His Father had given it to Him. Further, He promises to go with us and to strengthen and encourage us

with this same power as we live our lives of service and witness so that we may share the Good News through which God brings others into His family of believers. In Eph. 1:15–23, Paul refers to this great power as the same power that raised Christ from the dead and seated Him at His right hand in the heavenly realms. We share in this greatest of all power and authority as members of the church—the body of which Christ Himself is the head.

3. If by the power of the Holy Spirit we desire to dedicate our lives to Him who died for us and rose again, that desire and commitment includes yielding to His plan and purpose for living the Christian life as He has provided it for us in His Holy Word. God's Word is the source and norm for what God's people believe and teach, the first source for direction, encouragement, and strength in the face of challenging life situations and dilemmas.

4. In discussing this question with the group, stress that God blesses and encourages His people through the positive influence of others. At times, God even blesses us through unbelieving authorities who provide for our protection and care. Encourage participants to give specific examples from their own lives of these blessings.

Vision

During This Week

Urge participants to read and complete one or more of the suggested activities during the coming week.

Closing Worship

Sing or speak together stanzas 1, 3, and 7 of "All Hail the Power" (*LW* 272), as printed in the Study Guide.

Scripture Lessons for Next Sunday

Assign the appointed lessons for the Seventeenth Sunday after Pentecost.

Session 2

Seventeenth Sunday
after Pentecost

Genesis 50:15–21; Romans 14:5–9; Matthew 18:21–35

Focus

Theme: *Full Forgiveness*

Law/Gospel Focus

Read aloud the Law/Gospel focus.

Objectives

Invite volunteers to read aloud the lesson objectives.

Opening Worship

Lead the group using the responsive prayer provided.

Introduction

Read or invite a volunteer to read the introductory paragraphs to the group. Invite participants to contribute other examples of relatively insignificant incidents leading to major and lengthy conflicts and the disruption of relationships. After a brief period of comments and sharing, continue with the discussion questions.

1. (And 2.) Accept participants' comments. Answers will probably center on human sinfulness as the ultimate source of the desire to seek vengeance when others have wronged us. Comment that back and forth attempts to even the score only end in an escalation of actions until one or the other side either stops or seeks to reconcile. As the proverb indicates everybody loses when seeking revenge, including the initiator of the action to get even. Negative actions harm both the doer as well as the receiver. Looking for opportunities to get even keeps the relationship digressing in a negative direction and robs participants from directing their

energies in ways that would build up both the individuals and the relationships.

3. Answers will vary. Perhaps at times we are led to the mistaken notion that God needs us to do His work of retribution for Him. Mention that Jesus teaches us a better way to respond to those who have hurt us—one that transcends our natural response. He says, "You have heard that it was said, 'Eye for eye, and tooth for tooth.' But I tell you, Do not resist an evil person. If someone strikes you on the right cheek, turn to him the other also. And if someone wants to sue you and take your tunic, let him have your cloak as well. If someone forces you to go one mile, go with him two miles. Give to the one who asks you, and do not turn away from the one who wants to borrow from you.

"You have heard that it was said, 'Love your neighbor and hate your enemy.' But I tell you: Love your enemies and pray for those who persecute you, that you may be sons of your Father in heaven. He causes His sun to rise on the evil and the good, and sends rain on the righteous and the unrighteous. If you love those who love you, what reward will you get? Are not even the tax collectors doing that? And if you greet only your brothers, what are you doing more than others? Do not even pagans do that? Be perfect, therefore, as your heavenly Father is perfect" (Matt. 5:43–48).

Inform

If participants have not read the Scripture lessons before class, read each in turn as it is discussed. Comment that each of these three portions of God's Word help us to understand how God would have us build relationships with others including those who have wronged us.

1. Joseph's brothers plotted to kill him, stripped him of the beautiful robe he had been given as a gift from his father, threw him into a cistern, and finally, sold him into slavery for 20 pieces of silver. To cover up their evil deed, they dipped Joseph's robe in goat's blood to get their father to believe that Joseph had been killed, torn apart, and eaten by some ferocious animal. Joseph's brothers acted with little regard for his life; they might have murdered him had not Judah and Reuben dissuaded them.

2. It appears that Joseph's brothers concocted a story that Jacob's deathbed request was for them to ask Joseph to forgive them.

After telling Joseph about this supposed request, the brother's proceeded to ask Joseph's forgiveness. But God had given Joseph the ability to look upon the events of his life through the eyes of faith. Joseph recognized God's saving work on behalf of His people even during the lowest moments of Joseph's life, when due to the hateful actions of his brothers, he was forced to endure slavery, false accusation, and imprisonment. Through it all, Joseph professed, God was setting the stage in order to present something good—the salvation of his people. Refer participants also to Rom. 8:28.

3. Paul advised the Christians at Rome to respect and allow for individual differences. Some will regard one day more sacred than others, as in honoring the Old Testament Sabbath; others will hold to the importance of dedicating every day to the Lord. Likewise with respect to eating meat that had been sacrificed to idols. The important consideration in this and any other daily decision is that we focus on God and His will for us. Individuals who do so may reach differing conclusions yet each may act on his or her decision to the glory of God. Paul goes on to acclaim God as the Lord of all—the dead and the living. For those who by faith belong to Him are His whether we live or die.

4. Accept participants' responses. Paul explains (v. 9) that Christ died and returned to life so that He might be the Lord of both the dead and the living. Underscore the confidence we can have, even in death, knowing that our Savior and Friend has gone through death before us and is by our side even as we walk through death to the new life that awaits us in the world to come, where we will know Jesus in a more complete and perfect way.

5. Answers will vary somewhat. Jesus is Lord of the kingdom of grace—all believers, those living on earth and those already transformed to heavenly glory. In another vein, Jesus is Lord over the kingdom of power—He rules over those who walk in the light of life and also over unbelievers, those who remain spiritually dead and remain in the darkness of sin.

6. Peter may have been looking for a loophole in God's Law, whereby he could rightly refuse to forgive someone who continually offended him. Peter's question shows the focus of his concern to be on the overt act of forgiving rather than on the inclination of his heart toward the offender. Jesus' parable emphasizes true forgiveness and its origin in a forgiving heart (v. 35).

7. Jesus directs our attention to the magnitude and generosity associated with the forgiveness we have received. He contrasts it to the relatively insignificant quantity of forgiveness we are required to share with others. Underscore Christ's unlimited forgiveness as the power behind our ability to forgive from the heart those who have sinned against us. The annals of the Christian experience evidence amazing examples of God's forgiving power in the lives of His people. One Christian man, for instance, not only forgave, but adopted as his son the one who executed his son during an Asian war; this adopted son was converted and became a Christian pastor. Invite participants to contribute other examples from their own knowledge and experience.

Connect

Read the introductory paragraphs to the group. Then proceed with the questions.

1. Allow time for participants to work independently to complete this activity. Invite comments from the group that may have been generated by this exercise. Comment that forgiving—and especially forgiving from the heart does not occur naturally or easily. Stress that failures to forgive from the heart are among those sins for which Christ paid the ultimate price.

2. Encourage discussion about the obstacles on the road to forgiving others fully. Comment on the "I can forgive but I can't forget" that indicates holding on to a portion of the offense rather than forgiving it completely. Emphasize the work of the Holy Spirit through Word and Sacrament, generating within us the power and desire to grow in our ability to forgive.

3. Invite participants to share with the group the meaning of Christ's full and complete forgiveness for their lives. Generate enthusiasm by sharing what Jesus' forgiveness means personally to you. Emphasize the mercy and compassion of the Lord, new every morning. Comment that Christianity is all about starting over in the knowledge that Christ has wiped the slate clean for us. We need no long carry the weight and burden of the sins for which Jesus has paid the penalty. In our Baptism we are reminded that our sins are buried in Christ.

Vision

During This Week

Urge participants to read and complete one or more of the suggested activities during the coming week.

Closing Worship

Sing or speak together "I Lay My Sins on Jesus" (*LW* 366) as printed in the Study Guide.

Scripture Lessons for Next Sunday

Assign the appointed lessons for the Eighteenth Sunday after Pentecost.

Session 3

Eighteenth Sunday
after Pentecost

Isaiah 55:6–9; Philippians 1:1–11, 19–27; Matthew 20:1–16

Focus

Theme: *Not by Work*

Law/Gospel Focus

Read aloud the Law/Gospel focus.

Objectives

Invite volunteers to read aloud the lesson objectives.

Opening Worship

Lead the group using the responsive prayer provided.

Introduction

Read or invite a volunteer to read the introductory paragraphs to the group. Invite participants' comments. Continue with the discussion questions in this section. If no one mentions it, you may comment that many find their identity and sense of purpose and fulfillment in their work. While aspects of this perspective are healthy and faithfulness toward our life's vocation and its daily tasks can be done to the honor and glory of God, work is but one dimension in a healthy person's life.

1. Accept all participant's responses. Help the group to focus on both the positives and negatives associated with work.

2. Answers will vary somewhat. Most likely participants will expect work to give them a sense of fulfillment, providing an opportunity to make a contribution through the work itself and through the means of support work provides for both the worker and his or her family. Thus, work offers the means to accomplish life's goals

and dreams. Also, many value their work because of the friendships they have established in the workplace. Realistically, most expect workdays to be of varying kinds, those that are productive and satisfying as well as those that are filled with disappointment and frustration.

3. "Workaholism" takes its toll on family relationships, friendships, mental and physical health, and most certainly on spiritual vitality. Many people feel the need to justify their existence on earth through constant work. Accept participant responses in a nonjudgmental way.

Inform

If participants have not read the Scripture lessons before class, read each in turn as it is discussed. Comment that each of these passages can be seen as focusing not on our work and its rewards, but rather on God and the rewards he freely and abundantly provides us despite our lack of worthiness or merit. Continue with a discussion of the questions.

1. "Seek the Lord" is God's continual and gracious invitation to turn from sin and its confounding and controlling influences that in the end lead only to despair and condemnation to the one who has redeemed us from sin and prepared a special place for us as a son or daughter in His kingdom. Along with the invitation is a qualifier, "while He may be found." These words remind us that, because of sin, the Gospel may not always be so popular and prevalent among those living in a given area. Consider, for example, the birthplace of the Reformation. In Europe today, a declining number of people even claim to be Christians. Churches are valued largely for their historical importance rather than as places large active congregations gather regularly for worship. Some refer to today's society as having entered the post-Christian era. Despite these foreboding truths God remains always near to those who love and trust in Him. He promises never to leave and always to support, encourage, and strengthen us through the means of grace.

2. Samuel testified of God, "He who is the Glory of Israel does not lie or change His mind; for He is not a man, that He should change His mind" (1 Sam. 15:29). God is faithful to His Word; those of judgment as well as those of promise. Moreover, His

standards transcend those of mortals. At the selection of young David as Israel's next king, God told Samuel, "The Lord does not look at the things man looks at. Man looks at the outward appearance, but the Lord looks at the heart" (1 Sam. 16:7). 1 Cor. 1:21–25 provides further insight into the mysterious ways of God.

> For since in the wisdom of God the world through its wisdom did not know him, God was pleased through the foolishness of what was preached to save those who believe. Jews demand miraculous signs and Greeks look for wisdom, but we preach Christ crucified: a stumbling block to Jews and foolishness to Gentiles, but to those whom God has called, both Jews and Greeks, Christ the power of God and the wisdom of God. For the foolishness of God is wiser than man's wisdom, and the weakness of God is stronger than man's strength. (1 Cor. 1:21–25)

3. Paul prays with joy because of the partnership in the Gospel he shares with the believers at Philippi. He is confident that God will continue the gift of faith in those who belong to Him. Further, he prays for the spiritual growth of the believers, so that they "may be able to discern what is best and may be pure and blameless until the day of Christ, filled with the fruit of righteousness that comes through Jesus Christ—to the glory and praise of God" (Phil. 1:10–11). As Paul is directed, empowered, and motivated by the Spirit of the living God, his chief concern is the spiritual welfare of his friends at Philippi.

4. Paul expresses thankfulness to God and true delight at the working of the Gospel in the lives of the people. Paul comments that whether he is in chains or defending and confirming the Gospel, all the faithful share God's grace together with him (v. 7). He prays that this growth will continue "to the glory and praise of God" (v. 11). These words speak the blessings of Christian friendships—the extra closeness brought to human relationships in the knowledge that we are together now and will be together forever in the more perfect existence in our Savior's presence yet to come. Paul comments, "It is right for me to feel this way about all of you, since I have you in my heart" (v. 7).

5. As believers struggle with the challenges and obligations of both the work-a-day world and family life, they are strengthened and encouraged by the power of the Gospel to bear their burden while at the same time living and witnessing to the hope they

have within them. Yet one day our Savior will call us home. In His presence we will enjoy the perfect bliss, contentment, and satisfaction only hinted at during our best of times in this life. As we look forward to heaven, the author of Hebrews encourages us to "fix our eyes on Jesus, the author and perfecter of our faith, who for the joy set before Him endured the cross, scorning its shame, and sat down at the right hand of the throne of God. Consider Him who endured such opposition from sinful men, so that you will not grow weary and lose heart" (Heb. 12:2–3).

6. Paul encourages believers to live lives faithful to the Gospel so that their lives would be a witness to the power of Christ at work in them.

7. God gives graciously and generously. He is not bound by our human ideas about fairness or worthiness. He loves us and provides us with a grace as amazing as it is abundant. The parable illustrates God's desire to forgive (Is. 55:7) and His marvelous ways which are beyond the human ability to comprehend (vv. 8–9).

Connect

Use the questions in this section to underscore the limitless, incomprehensible love which moved God to send His Son to live, die, and rise again to earn forgiveness of sins and a new and eternal life for us and to make these gifts available to all people completely free of charge without our having worked for, deserved, or in any way having merited them.

1. Abraham is justified by faith, and not by works. The promise of God came to him, and he welcomed God's gifts. We are Abraham's heirs today by faith, that is, we share in the same faith of Abraham: we believe God's promise of love and forgiveness in Christ, and faith is credited to us as righteousness.

2. Answers will vary. Direct the participants to formulate a confession that acknowledges all of our past accomplishments and efforts pale in contrast to the abundant mercy of Christ.

3. Popular work ethic proclaims success to those who plan well, work hard, put the customer first, respect and motivate those who work with them, are always on the lookout for a cheaper, faster, more expedient way for developing and offering a product or providing a service. The Gospel of Jesus offers a contrasting perspective: God gives eternal life to all who have and possess faith which is also His free gift. We can't earn or in any way qualify ourselves to receive it.

4. Perhaps work always does come before success. With regard to the Gospel, however, it is Christ who has done all of the work for us. We are the recipients of the extreme efforts He extended in order to restore the Father/child relationship between holy God and fallen humanity.

Vision

During This Week

Urge participants to read and complete one or more of the suggested activities.

Closing Worship

Sing or speak together stanzas 1, 2, and 4 of "My Hope Is Built on Nothing Less" (*LW* 368) as printed in the Study Guide.

Scripture Lessons for Next Sunday

Assign the appointed lessons for the Nineteenth Sunday after Pentecost.

Session 4

Nineteenth Sunday after Pentecost

Ezekiel 18:1–4, 25–32; Philippians 2:1–5 (6–11);
Matthew 21:28–32

══ Focus ══

Theme: *Excuses, Excuses!*

Law/Gospel Focus

Read aloud the Law/Gospel focus.

Objectives

Invite volunteers to read aloud the lesson objectives.

Opening Worship

Lead the group using the responsive prayer provided.

Introduction

Read or invite a volunteer to read the introductory paragraphs aloud. Then move immediately to the discussion questions.

1. Someone has said that we live in a society where everyone wants to blame others and no one is willing to take the responsibility. Following are but a few examples: a woman successfully sues a fast-food restaurant after she spills a cup of coffee purchased there and burns herself; calling themselves victims of an oppressive society, drug addicts refuse treatment while continuing to collect a government assistance check; adults blame the home in which they were raised for the difficulties that plague them and keep them from reaching their full potential; school children blame parents, teachers, administrators, curriculum, and society in general for their lack of success in school. Invite participants to give examples of excuses they have heard or have found themselves offering to others.

2. Blaming others elevates the blamer above the level of failure to the status of victim—someone who could have excelled had not insuperable forces retained them. In addition, many "victims" advance what they believe is their right to receive compensation for the losses they have incurred.

3. Invite participants' comments. Answers may vary. Some may advance the notion that making excuses for others is one way to "put the best construction on things" as Luther reminds us to do in the explanation to the Eighth Commandment. Making excuses for ourselves, however, may keep us from either owning up to our sinfulness, repenting of our sins, and turning to God in Christ for forgiveness, power, and a new beginning.

Inform

If participants have not read the Scripture lessons before class, read each in turn as it is discussed.

1. The proverb "The fathers eat sour grapes, and the children's teeth are set on edge" refers to the mistaken belief that children are not to be held responsible for sin because it has been handed down to them by their forefathers. Just as no son ever simply received genetically the mighty biceps a blacksmith builds over years of hammering iron over a forge, no child can escape the consequence of sin in his or her life simply because sin in indigenous to the human condition and is therefore excusable. Each is held accountable for his or her own sin. In the words of Jeremiah, "Whoever eats sour grapes—his own teeth will be set on edge" (Jer. 31:30).

2. Ezekiel's Old Testament audience believed that if a person who lived an outwardly righteous life fell into sin, he should still not suffer punishment because of his righteous accomplishments (vv. 25–26). They thought it unfair that a wicked person could turn from his sin in true repentance and be saved (vv. 27–28).

3. Repentance means owning our sinfulness, expressing contrition over our sins, and turning to God for His forgiving, restoring, life-renewing strength, provided freely to all through the merits of Christ. Such is the will of God for all people everywhere (1 Tim. 2:4). By God's grace and the power of the Holy Spirit repentance leads to a new life filled with a new set of goals and priorities, one that evidences the fruit of the Spirit (Gal. 5:22–23) in the good

works and righteous acts God has prepared in advance for us to do (Eph. 2:10).

4. To be like-minded as the people of God involves celebrating God's goodness to us in Christ Jesus, encouraging one another in this Good News, and joining together in the mission and ministry of the fellowship of believers to which they belong. "One spirit and one purpose" is lived out in Christian congregations as we confess together our common faith in Him who died for us and rose again, as we partake together the means of grace, and join together in corporate worship, as we pray for and encourage one another, and as we plan and work together to share the Good News of Jesus with all who do not yet believe.

5. Though very God, Jesus emptied Himself of His godliness, taking upon Himself the form of His created being. Humbling Himself, He took our load of guilt because of our sin, lived a perfect life in our place, and died a horrible death on the cross to pay the penalty all sins deserved. But though He died, He rose again from the dead to proclaim the victory He had won over sin, death, and all forces of evil. Now, though still both God and man, He is exalted in heavenly glory where God has presented Him with a name that is above every name. One day every knee will bow before Him—including the knee of those stiff in unbelief—and every tongue will recognize Him for who He claims to be.

6. Genuine humility in the life of Christians recognizes our sinfulness. In humility and faith we turn to God for help and receive the crown of salvation (Ps. 149:4). God gives grace to those who come to Him humble and contrite because of sin (Prov. 3:34). God promises that whoever humbles himself like a child—trusting in His mercy rather than our own power or accomplishments—is the greatest in the kingdom of heaven (Matt. 18:4). Exalting ourselves works against the salvation God wishes to provide us; persons with true humility, which is characteristic of a truly repentant spirit, are exalted as God richly showers His abundant blessings upon His faithful followers (Matt. 23:12). Humility evidences the working of the Spirit in the life of the believer (Titus 3:2 and 1 Peter 5:5–6).

7. (And 8.) The first son at first refused to go into the vineyard to work and later changed his mind. He represents the repentant sinner—the one who recognized his sinfulness and turned to God for the righteousness available only through Christ Jesus.

The second son said he would go and work but did not do. The second son represents those who trust in their own righteousness and do not receive true righteousness from God because they refuse to own up to their sinfulness and repent. Jesus further differentiates between the two groups when he said, "Tax collectors and prostitutes [the social dregs of the day] are entering the kingdom of God ahead of you" (Matt. 21:31). Mere assent to God or to things spiritual will in the end provide nothing. Only those who repent and by faith receive Christ's righteousness will enter the kingdom of God.

Connect

Read the brief introductory paragraph to the group. Stress God's action on our part making our salvation totally the result of Christ's saving action. Continue with the discussion questions.

1. Rights refers to our just expectations of those around us and of the society in which we live. Responsibility refers to our ownership of the realities in which we find ourselves. Although we have inherited sin from our forefathers, each of us must assume responsibility for his or her own sin, recognize our total lack of rights and privileges before the throne of almighty God, confess our sins, and receive the free and abundant forgiveness and blessing He generously offers to us through Christ our Lord. The Law of God is for "lawbreakers and rebels, the ungodly and sinful, the unholy and irreligious; for those who kill their fathers or mothers, for murderers, for adulterers and perverts, for slave traders and liars and perjurers—and for whatever else is contrary to the sound doctrine" (1 Tim. 1:9–10), to bring us sinners to a knowledge of our sinfulness (Rom. 3:20). As Paul says, he "would not have known what sin was except through the law" (Rom. 7:7). The Gospel, on the other hand, is "the power of God for the salvation of everyone who believes" (Rom. 1:16).

2. Answers will vary somewhat. Because of our sinful nature, accepting responsibility for our failures is seldom easy, even for the people of God. But as the Spirit of God works in our lives through Word and Sacrament, He develops within us a continual desire to confess our sins, provides us with the assurance that these and all others sins have already been paid for, and fortifies

in us the resolve to rededicate ourselves to Him who died for us and rose again. As God's people, when we feel convicted because of our sins we can rejoice knowing that Christ's forgiveness has covered them, having removed their penalty.

3. Stress that Jesus' atoning work for us was to free us from all guilt. Having embraced Christ's forgiveness we can let go of all that would cause us to feel guilty and condemned. "We set our hearts at rest in [God's] presence whenever our hearts condemn us. For God is greater than our hearts, and He knows everything" (1 John 3:19–20). Rom. 8:1 reminds us that there is no condemnation for those who are in Christ Jesus. For Christ Himself intercedes for us at the right hand of God and nothing can separate us from His love (Rom. 8:31–34). We have the assurance of His forgiving love (Ps. 32:5).

Vision

During This Week

Urge participants to read and complete one or more of the suggested activities.

Closing Worship

Sing or speak together stanzas 1, 2, 3, and 6 of "The Law of God Is Good and Wise" (*LW* 329) as printed in the Study Guide.

Scripture Lessons for Next Sunday

Assign the appointed lessons for the Twentieth Sunday after Pentecost.

Session 5

Twentieth Sunday after Pentecost

Isaiah 5:1–7; Philippians 3:12–21; Matthew 21:33–43

Focus

Theme: *Grapes of Wrath ... and Grace*

Law/Gospel Focus

Read aloud the Law/Gospel focus.

Objectives

Invite volunteers to read aloud the lesson objectives.

Opening Worship

Lead the group using the responsive prayer provided.

Introduction

Read or invite a volunteer to read the introductory paragraphs to the group. Continue immediately with a discussion of the questions in this section.

1. Answers will vary. Participants are likely to suggest the following images associated with the word *garden:* lush, well-cared-for plots of earth; carefully planned arrangements of plants with each plant especially chosen and placed for the contribution it makes to the whole garden; a variety of plants, complimenting yet contrasting one another with regard to foliage, types and colors of flowers, and height and shape.

2. A careful gardener plants, transplants, prunes, weeds, fertilizes, waters, and trims plants. The gardener protects the plants and their harvest from insects, parasites, birds, and from forces of nature that may damage or destroy them. He or she usually takes time to enjoy the growth, beauty, and produce the garden provides, delighting in the lush array of plant life the garden has produced under his or her tender care.

3. Vineyards were important in the ancient world as a source for oil, wine, and fruit—staples of life.

Inform

If participants have not read the Scripture lessons before class, read each in turn as it is discussed. If you choose, refer to the garden imagery as you discuss each of the lessons. In the Old Testament and New Testament lessons the connection is obvious. The Epistle shows us as the people how, by the power of the Holy Spirit, we may grow in Christ as God's nurtured and sustained plants, until such time as we become a harvest for eternal life and happiness in our Savior's presence in heaven.

1. Verse 1 and the first part of verse 2 tell of the vineyard, planted on a fertile hill. The gardener "dug it up and cleared it of stones and planted it with the choicest vines. He built a watchtower in it and cut out a winepress as well." The second half of verse 2 and the remainder of the verses in the reading speak of God's judgment against His people. The gardener looked for a crop of good grapes but found only bad fruit after he had done all he could for the garden. The gardener speaks his plan. He will take away the garden's protective hedge and wall and make it a trampled and destroyed wasteland which is neither pruned nor cultivated and briers and thorns will grow there. Further he will command the clouds not to rain on it. In verse 7 the parable is clearly explained, "The vineyard of the LORD Almighty is the house of Israel, and the men of Judah are the garden of His delight. And He looked for justice, but saw bloodshed; for righteousness, but heard cries of distress."

2. God gave the people of Israel their home. He abundantly provided for them, satisfying their physical and spiritual needs. He Himself stood as a watchtower so as to protect a productive garden. He provided Israel victory over their heathen enemies (weeding them out of Israel by the strength of His power). In short, God provided His people with all they needed to bear much fruit in the lives they lived for Him.

3. Nathan told David the story of the rich man who though possessing abundant cattle and sheep, took a poor man's only lamb which was his pet and prepared it as food for a traveler who came to visit him. Nathan asked David to pronounce judgment against the rich

man and David did so without realizing Nathan was describing him. Similarly, God asks the people of Israel who would be most familiar with the plight of the owner of the vineyard what more He might have done for the vineyard (v. 4). The irony here is that God is setting the people of Israel up to pass judgment on themselves and their actions of unfaithfulness.

4. Paul says, "I press on toward the goal to win the prize for which God has called me heavenward in Christ Jesus" (Phil. 3:14). The past Paul talks about leaving behind includes a life of ignorance of Jesus and the gift of salvation He earned for Paul and everyone everywhere and persecution against the people of God. For Paul, as for all who trust in Jesus for salvation, the past is forgiven. It need not keep us from enjoying our new life in Christ today or hamper our efforts to press on with Christ in the new and eternal life that is ours by the power of the Holy Spirit.

5. Answers will vary. Christian maturity includes proclaiming Christ while "admonishing and teaching everyone with all wisdom, so that we may present everyone perfect in Christ" (Col. 1:28) "until we all reach unity in the faith and in the knowledge of the Son of God and become mature, attaining to the whole measure of the fullness of Christ" (Eph. 4:13). Stress Christian maturity as sanctification, the work of the Holy Spirit in the life of the believer through Word and Sacrament.

6. A person possessing an earthly mindset has the things of this life as his or her foremost concern. Such a person will express the following concerns: how can I provide comfort and security for myself and my loved one? how can I achieve satisfaction and success? how can I find happiness and fame? Those already possessing citizenship in heaven even as they live on earth have the freedom to concern themselves with things of true and eternal value, such as growing in a knowledge and love of God, possessing a concern for meeting the physical and especially the spiritual needs of others, and experiencing even now the blessings of the inheritance Christ as earned by them—including a peace that passes all understanding and a joy in Him that is not dependent on external supports.

7. In Jesus' parable tenants were to tend the garden that the landowner had planted with tender care. In Jesus' parable as well as in the Isaiah parable a winepress was dug and a watchtower built. In the Isaiah parable the vineyard represents God's people.

In Jesus' account the vineyard represents the kingdom of God. When in Jesus' parable, the owner sent servants (prophets) to collect the harvest, the tenants beat, killed, and stoned them. Finally, the owner sent his own son and the tenants took him and threw him out of the vineyard and killed him to get the inheritance. Jesus' question, "When the owner of the vineyard comes, what will he do to those tenants?" (Matt. 21:40) reminds us of the question in the Isaiah parable when God invites the people to pass judgment on the vineyard (Is. 5:4). In Matt. 21:42, Jesus identifies Himself as the stone, rejected by the builders, that has become the main supporting element (capstone) of the object under construction. Jesus is the foundation of the one true church—the only way of salvation. Jesus has made us His people, having bought us for Himself with His very life, and what He has done for us "is marvelous in our eyes" (Matt. 21:42).

Connect

Read or invite a volunteer to read aloud the introductory paragraphs in this section. Ask participants to share difficulties with growing things they have either observed or witnessed firsthand. Underscore the dynamic growing and producing power of the Gospel at work in the hearts and lives of those who belong to Christ. Ask for examples of dynamic growth and crop production in the lives of those carefully tended by the Holy Spirit. Continue with a discussion of the questions in this section.

1. God the Father, the Gardener, cuts off every branch that bears no fruit (removes evil from among the people of God), while every branch that does bear fruit He prunes so that it will be even more fruitful. God works in the lives of His people in the midst of their challenges, adversities, and strife, building a strong and hearty people able to weather the rigors of life planted in foreign soil while they look forward to the perfect habitat of heaven.

   Jesus the Vine is our conduit to life. He provides us with strength and nutrition. Through His Word He makes us clean (v. 3). Connected to Him God's people are able to bear much fruit; apart from Him, they can do nothing (v. 4).

   Jesus' disciples are the branches (v. 5). No branch can bear the fruit by itself. Neither can disciples bear the fruit of the Christian life unless they remain in Christ (v. 4). Apart from Jesus we can do nothing. If anyone does not remain in Christ, he is like a branch that is thrown away and withers; such branches are picked up, thrown into the fire and burned. But, Jesus says, if we remain in Him and His Word remains in us, we may ask whatever we wish, and it will be given us (v. 7). Jesus concludes that it is to His Father's glory that we bear much fruit, showing ourselves to be His disciples.

2. The fruit of the Spirit listed in Gal. 5:22 are as follows: love, joy, peace, patience, kindness, goodness, faithfulness, gentleness and self-control. These are the harvest the Spirit produces (and desires to produce to an ever-greater degree) in lives empowered by Him as He works through Word and Sacrament.

Vision

During This Week

Urge participants to read and complete one or both of the suggested activities.

Closing Worship

Sing or speak together stanzas 1, 3, 5, and 7 of "At the Name of Jesus" (*LW* 178) as printed in the Study Guide.

Scripture Lessons for Next Sunday

Assign the appointed lessons for the Twenty-first Sunday after Pentecost.

Session 6

Twenty-first Sunday
after Pentecost

Isaiah 25:6–9; Philippians 4:4–13; Matthew 22:1–10 (11–14)

Focus

Theme: *Abundant Life*

Law/Gospel Focus

Read aloud the Law/Gospel focus.

Objectives

Invite volunteers to read aloud the lesson objectives.

Opening Worship

Lead the group using the responsive prayer provided.

Introduction

Read or invite a volunteer to read the introductory paragraphs to the group. Continue immediately with a discussion of the questions in this section.

1. Answers will vary. Participant responses are likely to reflect some of the following thoughts: In a relatively short period of time God has raised our nation from a frontier outpost to one of most industrial and technological modern countries of the world. He has given us a standard of living never before experienced in history. He has given us freedom of expression so that we may openly live, profess, and share the saving faith in our society. Through technology and know-how we have immediate access to information, improved communication, better medical care, and ease of travel.

2. Allow participants to share a time God's abundant provision for them was especially meaningful. If possible, "prime the pump" by sharing a time when you especially appreciated God's generosity in your life.

Inform

If participants have not read the Scripture lessons before class, read each in turn as it is discussed.

1. Examples in Isaiah 25 that pertain to meeting basic human needs include God's mighty power in accomplishing this purpose. The Lord has been a refuge for the poor and needy, a shelter from the storm and a shade from the heat (vv. 4–5). God will provide us with a festival-like existence, a banquet of the finest food and drink. He will swallow death forever, wiping away the tears from all faces, and removing the disgrace of His people from all the earth (vv. 6–8). Verse 9 speaks the salvation we all will enjoy through faith in Him who defeated death for us (on Calvary's tree) and of the joy His salvation brings to us.

2. Mountains, especially for those living in ancient times, symbolized the dwelling place of the deity. The image of the feast prepared on the mountain (v. 6) is a reference to heaven (Rev. 19:9). Here God will wipe away all tears from all faces (Rev. 7:17).

3. The words of 1 Cor. 15:54–56 praise Christ for the result His work has yielded—the swallowing up of death in victory. Although Christians still must face physical death, its real power was extinguished when Jesus overcame death on our behalf.

4. Jesus lived, died, and rose again for all people, including Paul. By faith Paul had come to know Jesus as His personal Lord and Savior. Plus, God had given Paul an important role to fulfill as His disciple. Through the working of the Holy Spirit in his life, Paul had come to know the joy of salvation in all of life's circumstances. Although he was forced to endure many hardships for the sake of the Gospel, he knew the peace and joy in Christ that are not dependent upon external conditions. That was the joy and peace Paul and Silas experienced as they sang hymns while locked in a Philippian jail (Acts 16:25). Knowing by faith the riches of God's grace, as Paul did, Christians of all time have been able to rejoice in the Lord.

5. Invite participants to help you make a brief list of thoughts and actions that qualify according to the description provided in Phil. 4:8. Write their suggestions on the chalkboard or on a large piece of newsprint. Help participants discover that these kinds of thoughts and actions build up and encourage, and, when done in response to the Gospel, help us provide a positive witness to

those around us of the love of Christ operative in the things we think, say, and do.

6. Paul says that he has known what it is to be in need and what it is to have plenty. The secret of contentment, Paul says, rests regardless of circumstances in knowing he can do everything through Christ, who gives him strength. Stress that the gifts of joy, peace, and contentment come to the lives of God's people as the Holy Spirit provides them through the means of grace.

7. The king originally invites those that would normally have been expected to attend the wedding banquet of the king's son. The king displays hospitality and patience in repeatedly sending servants to urge those invited with the message that the banquet is ready. Those invited refuse (v. 3). They pay the servants no attention (v. 5). Some go as far as to seize the king's servants, mistreat them, and kill them.

8. The king, considering the refusal of the initial invitees, sends his servants out again. This time they are to gather in all the people they can find, both good and bad, so that the wedding hall is filled with guests. By this action the king shows himself to regard all prospective attendees equally—he does not discriminate in any way.

9. Point out that the custom in ancient times was for the host of a banquet to provide the guest with appropriate attire. Therefore the refusal to dress appropriately does not reflect simply a lack of means on the part of the guests. Rather it indicates a disdain for the host who has freely provided everything, including the apparel befitting a proper wedding banquet. The man without proper apparel represents those who reject God's gracious invitation even as they are associated with those who have faith. Christ has earned righteousness (wedding garment) for all through His atoning work. Nevertheless, only those who receive it in faith will be saved.

Connect

Introduce and allow time for participants to read silently the words of "Jerusalem the Golden" and to complete item 1. Then review responses to item 1 and continue with a discussion of the remaining items in this section.

1. Circled words or phrases providing other names for heaven will include but are not necessarily limited to the following: *Jerusalem the golden; halls of Zion; the pastures of the blessed; sweet and blessed country; the home of God's elect; sweet and blessed country that eager hearts expect; that dear land of rest.* Underlined words or phrases that describe the blessings of heaven may include, though are not necessarily limited to, the following: *with milk and honey blest; beneath your contemplation sink heart and voice oppressed; what radiancy of glory; what bliss beyond compare; conjubilant with song; bright with many an angel and all the martyr throng; the prince is ever in them; the daylight is serene; decked in glorious sheen; there is the throne of David and there, from care released, the shout of those who triumph, the song of those who feast; they, who with their leader have conquered in the fight, forever and forever are clad in robes of white.*

2. Rev. 21:1–8 describes the new Jerusalem as a beautiful bride prepared for her husband. Here God will dwell with His people, He will wipe every tear from their eyes, and there will be no more death or mourning or crying or pain, for the old order of things will have passed away. God will freely give this inheritance to all. Revelation 22:1–5 further describes heaven as the majesty we will enjoy forever at the throne of the Lamb. "No longer will there be any curse. The throne of God and of the Lamb will be in the city, and His servants will serve Him. They will see His face, and His name will be on their foreheads. There will be no more night. They will not need the light of a lamp or the light of the sun, for the Lord God will give them light. And they will reign for ever and ever" (Rev. 22:3–5).

3. Allow participants to share the promises of eternal life in heaven that are especially meaningful and comforting to them. Encourage them to share the anticipation of a completely happy and perfect existence at the throne of the maker and ruler of the universe, who is also our personal Savior and best and truest friend.

Vision

During This Week

Urge participants to read and complete at least one of the suggested activities.

Closing Worship

Sing or speak together stanzas 1, 2, 4, and 5 of "Jesus Shall Reign" (*LW* 312) as printed in the Study Guide.

Scripture Lessons for Next Sunday

Assign the appointed lessons for the Twenty-second Sunday after Pentecost.

Session 7

Twenty-second Sunday
after Pentecost

Isaiah 45:1–7; 1 Thessalonians 1:1–5a; Matthew 22:15–21

Focus

Theme: *Chosen by God*

Law/Gospel Focus

Read aloud the Law/Gospel focus.

Objectives

Invite volunteers to read aloud the lesson objectives.

Opening Worship

Lead the group using the responsive prayer provided.

Introduction

Read or invite a volunteer to read the introductory paragraphs to the group. Continue immediately with a discussion of the questions in this section.

1. Allow participants to share recent occurrences that came about as the result of a choice that surprised them. Be prepared in advance to contribute a choice that surprised you. Many will remember, for example, the surprise over the announcement that John F. Kennedy's widow, Jacqueline Kennedy, had chosen to marry the much-older billionaire tycoon, Aristotle Onassis. Take care not to spend too much time on either this or the next item.

2. Encourage discussion of most unusual choices—those that took family, friends, and co-workers by surprise. Share the most unusual choice you ever made. Lead the group to the realization that individually and as a society, life is full of surprises.

Inform

If participants have not read the Scripture lessons before class, read each in turn as it is discussed.

1. Point out that throughout history God has provided for His people through the care and generosity of secular—even unbelieving —rulers. Pharaoh at the time of Joseph, for example, made Joseph second in command of all Egypt. Therefore God saved Joseph and through Joseph the whole Israelite nation from starvation. Later, at the time of Exodus, God made the people of Israel rich by arranging for the Egyptians to give them money and jewelry to carry with them on their escape. As God's people, we do well to thank God for our rulers and obey them as instruments of God for the care, protection, and security of His people.

2. The mission of Cyrus is one of judgment against the enemies of the people of God. God promises to empower Cyrus, "whose right hand I take hold of to subdue nations ... and to strip kings of their armor, to open doors before him so that gates will not be shut." God promises to go before Cyrus to "level the mountains ... break down gates of bronze, and cut through bars of iron"— images that show the awesome magnitude of God's almighty power at work in this pagan king and the forces under his control for the ultimate benefit of the people of God.

3. God clearly states His purpose for Cyrus' life. "For the sake of Jacob my servant, of Israel My chosen, I summon you by name and bestow on you a title of honor, though you do not acknowledge Me. I am the LORD, and there is no other; apart from Me there is no God. I will strengthen you, though you have not acknowledged Me, so that from the rising of the sun to the place of its setting men may know there is none besides Me. I am the LORD, and there is no other. I form the light and create darkness, I bring prosperity and create disaster; I, the LORD, do all these things" (Is. 45:4–7).

4. Paul thanks God for the Thessalonian believers, mentioning them in prayer and remembering before God their work produced by faith, their labor prompted by love, and their endurance inspired by hope in our Lord Jesus Christ. Paul adds that he knows that God had chosen them because the Gospel came to the Thessalonians not simply with words but also with power. Stress the remarkable choice God made, not only in selecting Cyrus as His

instrument, but also in selecting people like the Thessalonians or like those of us who study and believe His Word today to be His own dear children.

5. The Thessalonians' "labor prompted by love" is described in 1 Corinthians 13, the love chapter, which talks about the love of God and how it is lived out in the lives of His people. Invite a volunteer to read the 13 verses of this beautiful chapter.

6. Asking the question of Jesus were both Pharisees and Herodians. The Pharisees were church leaders who opposed Roman rule. The Herodians, on the other hand, supported the Roman government. The question, "Is it right to pay taxes to Caesar or not?" could have been answered with either a yes or a no. Either answer could have gotten Jesus in trouble. A no would have meant Jesus opposed the government. A yes answer could have been construed as a favoring of the government over God and the church. Jesus' answer clears Him of either accusation.

7. Jesus' answer gives reference to the dual kingdoms in which God's people live and serve. We owe our first and primary allegiance to God (Acts 5:29), but we also serve God as we support and obey the government of the land in which we live (Rom. 13:1–7).

8. To the Romans Paul writes, "Everyone must submit himself to the governing authorities, for there is no authority except that which God has established. The authorities that exist have been established by God." Peter writes, "Submit yourselves for the Lord's sake to every authority instituted among men: whether to the king, as the supreme authority, or to governors, who are sent by Him to punish those who do wrong and to commend those who do right." Following this principle, Christians benefit themselves and the society in which they live as they work for the support and improvement of government.

Connect

Allow a minute or so for participants to read and reflect on the passages included in this section. They show God's amazing and remarkable choices of those He desired to make His own. Continue with a discussion of the questions.

1. Encourage participants to share their stories of how God worked even in times of trial and uncertainty to bless and provide for

people in their personal lives and in the lives they share together as members of your congregation.

2. Paul writes, "God chose the foolish things of the world to shame the wise ... the weak things of the world to shame the strong ... the lowly things of this world and the despised things—and the things that are not—to nullify the things that are, so that no one may boast before Him. It is because of Him that you are in Christ Jesus, who has become for us wisdom from God—that is, our righteousness, holiness, and redemption. Therefore, as it is written: 'Let him who boasts boast in the Lord.' "

3. According to this confession of faith, we can do no better than this: to look to God and place ourselves in His loving and caring hands when we face difficult and troublesome decisions. He always has our best interests at heart. He demonstrated the extent of His great love in sending Jesus to die in our place.

Vision

During This Week

Urge participants to read and complete at least one of the suggested activities.

Closing Worship

Sing or speak together the words of stanzas 1, 2, and 5 of "Lord of Glory, You Have Bought Us" (*LW* 402) as printed in the Study Guide.

Scripture Lessons for Next Sunday

Assign the appointed lessons for the Twenty-third Sunday after Pentecost.

Session 8

Twenty-third Sunday after Pentecost

Leviticus 19:1–2; 15–18; 1 Thessalonians 1:5b–10;
Matthew 22:34–40 (41–46)

Focus

Theme: *Principles, Priorities, Promises*

Law/Gospel Focus

Read aloud the Law/Gospel focus.

Objectives

Invite volunteers to read aloud the lesson objectives.

Opening Worship

Lead the group using the responsive prayer provided.

Introduction

Read or invite a volunteer to read the introductory paragraphs aloud. Continue immediately with a discussion of the questions in this section.

1. Some popular slogans are "Just do it" (Nike), "Obey Your Thirst" (Sprite), "Have You Had Your Break Today" (McDonalds), "Head for the Mountains" (Busch). Ask participants to identify other current advertising mottos.
2. At the time of this writing popular bumper stickers include those identifying the driver as the parent of a student of the month or an honor student at a given school. Others make a statement about abortion or some other issue controversial in American society. Still others give a Christian witness—"My boss Is a Jewish Carpenter" or "Jesus Loves You." Some are humorous, such as "If I'd Known Grandchildren Were This Much Fun, I'd Have Had Them First" or "Spending My Children's Inheritance" or "I

May Be Slow, but You're Following Me!" Others such as "Drive Carefully, Ex-wife (Mother-in-Law, etc.) in Truck." Encourage participants to share slogans or bumper stickers currently popular. Invite speculation about their messages.

3. Answers will vary.

4. Catchy slogans and slick advertisements make a ready impression and are therefore easily remembered. Mention that in the Old Testament reading for today God commands His people with the simple request, "Be holy because I, the Lord your God, am holy." This simple command sums up the entirety of God's Law. Point out that holiness is the theme of the entire book of Leviticus.

Inform

If participants have not read the Scripture lessons before class, read each in turn as it is discussed.

1. To be holy means to be perfect—without fault or defect. In Lev. 19:15–18 God demands holy behavior so His people "do not pervert justice ... show partiality to the poor or favoritism to the great, but judge your neighbor fairly. Do not ... [spread] slander ... do not do anything that endangers your neighbor's life. ... Do not hate your brother in your heart. Rebuke your neighbor frankly so you will not share in his guilt. Do not seek revenge or bear a grudge ... but love your neighbor as yourselves."

2. Leviticus 19 restates, explains, and amplifies the law of God, the Ten Commandments, first presented to the people of God in written form at Mount Sinai in the wilderness. Lev. 19:15 ("Do not pervert justice; do not show partiality ... or favoritism, ... but judge your neighbor fairly") pertains to Commandments 4–10. Verse 16 ("Do not go about spreading slander among your people") relates to Commandment 8 and ("Do not do anything that endangers your neighbor's life") Commandment 5. Verses 17 and 18 also relate to Commandments 4–10 and especially Commandment 5. ("Do not hate your brother in your heart. Rebuke your neighbor frankly so you will not share in his guilt. Do not seek revenge or bear a grudge against one of your people, but love your neighbor as yourself.")

3. In referring to the Thessalonians as "imitators ... of the Lord" Paul tells how the Gospel, which came to them "with power, with the Holy Spirit and with deep conviction" (1 Thess. 1:5)

evidenced itself in their lives. By the working of the Holy Spirit through the Gospel, God's people desire and are empowered to imitate Christ in lives of holiness, striving to serve and honor God in the goals, activities, and choices of their lives.

4. As the Spirit of God opened their hearts they turned from a life of idolatry and by the power of the Gospel began living their lives for Him who died for them and rose again. As the word of God spread, a social change swept the world of Paul's day; new converts began imitating those already in the faith, who in turn imitated Paul and other leaders of the day, who imitated Christ. They "turned to God from idols to serve the living and true God, and to wait for His Son from heaven, whom He raised from the dead—Jesus, who rescues us from the coming wrath."

5. By the power of the Holy Spirit God's people are led to live each day as it might be the last, with appreciation and gratitude to God for His many blessings and with a sense of urgency to share the saving truth with those who do not yet believe.

6. The love and sacrifice God made for His people was a total one. He empowers His people similarly to dedicate themselves to Him in all they are and have—a total commitment involving each individual's whole heart, soul, and strength.

7. God's selfless and unconditional expressions of love for the benefit of all people motivates His children to respond in a selfless regard, concern, and care for all others. The parable of the Good Samaritan shows that such love of others extends even to our enemies.

8. The two great commandments summarize the Law—God's requirements for us and for all people to fulfill. If we could love God and all others perfectly, we would be holy and would not need a Savior. Unfortunately, consideration of these two summaries of the Commandments shows us our failures under the Law. But the Gospel is the good news that Jesus has loved and continues to love God and others perfectly in our place. Also in our place, He died on a cruel wooden cross to pay the penalty our sins deserved. Thus these two great commandments summarize what God in Christ has done for us and our salvation.

Connect

The introductory portion of this section restates the main point of the previous section. Continue with a discussion of the questions.

1. Luther explains that the Spirit-driven response to the Gospel includes a desire to promote the kingdom of God, the knowledge and praise of His name, and the performance of His will by everybody. He adds that everyone benefits when this is accomplished. Underscore the emphasis on Christian living and outreach included in Luther's words, as a response to our Savior.

2. Jesus Himself is the source and strength of the disciples' love for one another (John 15:5). Christ's love is the touchstone of true love in the church (John 13:34–35) and the only true source of joy (John 15:11). John writes that love and obedience go hand in hand (John 15:9). Often we don't feel loving toward others. The power of the Gospel enables God's people to be and act lovingly even at times such as these. Jesus promises that God will hear and answer prayers of the faithful raised in His name (John 15:16–17).

3. Both the Romans and James passages list specific commandments; both refer to love as the summary and fulfillment of God's Law.

4. We love others and ourselves when we think of others and do for them what we would appreciate others doing for us if our circumstances were those of our neighbor.

Vision

During This Week

Urge participants to read and complete one or both of the suggested activities.

Closing Worship

Sing or speak together the words of "May We Your Precepts, Lord, Fulfill" (*LW* 389) as printed in the Study Guide.

Scripture Lessons for Next Sunday

Assign the appointed lessons for the Twenty-fourth Sunday after Pentecost.

Session 9

Twenty-fourth Sunday after Pentecost

Amos 5:18–24; 1 Thessalonians 4:13–18; Matthew 23:37–39

Focus

Theme: *A Cry for Life*

Law/Gospel Focus

Read aloud the Law/Gospel focus.

Objectives

Invite volunteers to read aloud the lesson objectives.

Opening Worship

Lead the group using the responsive prayer provided.

Introduction

Read or invite a volunteer to read the introductory paragraphs to the group. Point out that Lamentations provides the historical background for the lesson we will study in this lesson. Continue with a discussion of the questions.

1. Participants will most likely discuss the mourning that occurs on a national level over the death of a well-known political leader or society figure. Other examples include mourning that results from the devastation that occurs as the result of wars or natural disasters.

2. Encourage participants by sharing one or two examples from your own experience. Choose examples that illustrate the tragic consequences of our fallen condition and the ignorance and hopeless situations in which many of our contemporaries find themselves.

3. Jeremiah expressed concern that perhaps God has utterly rejected His people and that their condition places them beyond hope

of forgiveness and restitution thus ending the book of Lamentations on a sad and discouraging note. Feelings of hopelessness and despair often accompany the realization of sins and their effects in our lives. Fortunately, when we find ourselves in these times of discouragement and brokenheartedness, God in Christ stands ready and eager to assure us that our sins are forgiven and God's power is available to us to bring us the peace that passes all human understanding and to rebuild our broken lives. For God's "compassions never fail. They are new every morning; great is [God's] faithfulness" (Lam. 3:22b–23).

Inform

If participants have not read the Scripture lessons before class, read each in turn as it is discussed.

1. Israel expected a "day of the Lord" that included the elevation of the nation of Israel to a position of prominence and lordship over all other nations. Amos warned that this expectation was not to occur. The belief that we are worthy of more than we are being given is the very lie with which Satan first successfully tempted Adam and Eve in the Garden of Eden. People have tended to fall for the very same false notion ever since.

2. These two images—the man who escapes from the lion only to meet the bear and the man who enters his house and puts his hand on the wall of the house only to be bitten by a snake—both show people who anticipated rest and security only to be met instead with a calamity worse then they endured while in a period of anticipation. Point out the parallels to Israel and God's judgment and also to the judgment God will deliver at the end of the age.

3. God says His judgment will come upon the people because of the hollow and empty religious practices through which they sought to earn God's reward and favor. God uses the words *hate, cannot stand, will not accept, have no regard for, away with the noise,* and *will not listen* in reference to His disdain for heartless acts of worship offered by unbelieving people.

4. Accept participants' responses. This portion of Thessalonians points out that God's people sometimes mourn and grieve the loss of their loved ones as those who have no hope of enjoying the bliss of eternity in heaven with them.

5. Paul writes that at the Last Day the Lord Himself will come down from heaven with a loud command, with the voice of the archangel and with the trumpet call of God and the dead in Christ will rise first. After that, we who are still alive and are left will be caught up together with them in the clouds to meet the Lord in the air. And so we will be with the Lord forever (1 Thess. 4:16–18). To the Corinthians Paul writes, "We will not all sleep, but we will all be changed—in a flash, in the twinkling of an eye, at the last trumpet. For the trumpet will sound, the dead will be raised imperishable, and we will be changed. For the perishable must clothe itself with imperishable, and mortal with immortality (1 Cor. 15:51–53). The resurrection of Christ is the first of all those to follow (1 Cor. 15:23). This is the Christian hope and encouragement (1 Thess. 4:18).

6. At the final judgment only unbelievers have anything to fear. Believers can rejoice at the end of the world confident that Christ has paid in full the penalty of their sins. By faith they will be received into the home Jesus has ready for them in His eternal presence.

7. God's chosen people rejected and killed the prophets because they only wanted to hear about themselves as a people chosen by God. They did not want to hear about their sins and the consequences they would eventually have to endure because of them. Jesus weeps because if only they would have listened to the message of the prophets, repented, and received the message of the forgiveness God freely provided in Jesus they could have been saved and rescued from the horrible punishment they would otherwise, of necessity, be forced to endure.

8. Jesus' desire is always to call, save, and protect those who are lost just as a hen gathers her chick under the protection of her spreading wings.

Connect

Read or paraphrase the opening paragraphs for the group. Then continue with the discussion questions.

1. (And 2.) Accept participants' responses. Point out that Christians have reason to be both optimistic and pessimistic about the future. As sin continues, all of creation will continue to groan in anticipation

for the end (Rom. 8:21–22). We have cause to be concerned over the disregard for the things of God prevalent in our society and of the large numbers of people without faith in Jesus. Yet, as God's people we can be always optimistic since our Savior will remain with us regardless of what the future holds, and nothing—not even death—can separate us from His saving love (Rom. 8:37–39).

3. Bonhoefer laments the harsh conditions of the times in which he lives, asking God to care as a loving father for the wife and children for whom he is powerless to provide and care. Bonhoefer expresses also his deep faith: whether he lives or dies he remains with the Lord. He concludes in anticipation of the coming of his salvation and of the kingdom of God.

Vision

During This Week

Urge participants to read and complete at least one of the suggested activities.

Closing Worship

Sing or speak together stanzas 1, 3, and 4 of "The Church's One Foundation" (*LW* 289) as printed in the Study Guide.

Scripture Lessons for Next Sunday

Assign the appointed lessons for the Twenty-fifth Sunday after Pentecost.

Session 10

Twenty-fifth Sunday after Pentecost

Hosea 11:1–4, 8–9; 1 Thessalonians 5:1–11; Matthew 24:3–14

Focus

Theme: *On Guard!*

Law/Gospel Focus

Read aloud the Law/Gospel focus.

Objectives

Invite volunteers to read aloud the lesson objectives.

Opening Worship

Lead the group using the responsive prayer provided.

Introduction

Read or invite a volunteer to read the introductory paragraphs aloud. Continue with a discussion of the questions.

1. Accept participants' examples. People today must be on guard as they walk alone on dark streets at night, when they have car trouble, when they agree to a business deal that involves paying money before receiving anything in return, when welcoming strangers into their home, when choosing individuals, care centers, or schools to provide a service for their children, and when giving money to legitimate-sounding charities.

2. Parents, grandparents, and other adults concerned over the welfare of young people sometimes willingly share "on guard" expressions of caution out of a genuine desire to help young people avoid dangerous, costly, and even life-threatening mistakes. Similarly, a veteran at a task at the workplace often takes newer employees under his or her wing, advising them about problems that can be avoided.

Inform

If participants have not read the Scripture lessons before class, read each in turn as it is discussed.

1. God rescued His people Israel from the bondage of Egypt. He guided their escape as a pillar of cloud by day and a pillar of fire by night. Under the direction and leadership of Moses He divided the waters providing a dry passage across the sea in which He also drowned Pharaoh and his pursuing army. In the wilderness He provided Israel with water and food in miraculous ways. But the people's thankfulness and gratitude for His generous care were short-lived. They worshiped idols, complained about the sameness of their food, and grumbled about the leadership God had provided for them. Disregarding God and His promise to care for them, they expressed discouragement and disillusionment at the power and size of their enemies in the Promised Land.

2. God compares His love and concern for Israel to the love of a father for a wayward son. Regardless of the son's treatment of the father, he never stops hoping and looking for good in the relationship. In spite of the righteous anger God might pour out on Israel, He cannot help but be filled with compassion. Such is the unconditional love of God for His people.

3. Fickleness is a human characteristic, not a quality associated with God. Though people pledge their fidelity to God and then do whatever they feel compelled to do according to their own good pleasure or in response to the forces around them, God is faithful. His dedication to His people is completely reliable and unchangeable.

4. The Second Coming will occur without any advanced warning. Just as a thief enters when not expected, Jesus will come without announcing the specific time and date of His coming ahead. Paul's point is that people will be living as if the world will go on forever and then, unexpectedly, all things will end and a new era will begin.

5. Paul associates darkness with those who are spiritually asleep and caught up with activities (such as drunkenness) not conducive for those who are sons of the day. Associated with the day are alertness, self-control, faithfulness, love, and reliance upon Christ—the hope of our salvation. Participants are likely to affirm these qualities as equally appropriate and applicable for the times in which we live.

6. Allow participants to share. Perhaps it will be helpful to the discussion to define in advance false prophets as those who direct our attention away from Christ and Him crucified to themselves or to some other notion of salvation, including the idea—unfounded in Scripture—that everyone will get a second chance to repent and be saved after Christ comes again.

7. The end times capture the imagination of many who enjoy looking for the fulfillment of biblical prophecies in the world around them. While such interest and energies may be associated with Paul's concept of spiritual alertness, those interested in end times need to exercise caution not to become so caught up in looking for signs of the end they neglect their primary mission as disciples: to grow in faith and reach out with the saving Gospel to those who do not yet believe.

8. Jesus prepares the disciples by telling them that life in the last days will not be easy for the people of God. He warns that false prophets will deceive many people and that "because of the increase of wickedness, the love of most will grow cold." Nevertheless, He promises that those who remain firm to the end will be saved. He also underscores the mission and goal of the church—to preach the Gospel in the whole world as a testimony to all nations. After this has been accomplished, Christ says, the end will come. Mention that advancements in travel and communication technology signal the nearness of the end of all things.

Connect

Read or paraphrase the opening paragraphs for the group. Then continue with the discussion questions.

1. Accept participants' comments. Point out that the difficulties and struggles for the people of God, both those originating outside the church and those starting from within, are signs of the devil's last desperate attempts to win converts from the truth.

2. Allow a brief time for participants to reflect on their state of readiness. Mention that readiness can be as much the sign of a faithful Christian as it is the sign of an able soldier. Be sure to add however, that true readiness occurs only as the Holy Spirit equips us through the gift of faith He provides as He works in us through Word and Sacrament.

3. Encourage the group to respond to this question. Certainly, sharing information about the forces at work in society to undermine the Christian faith is one important aspect of readiness. Most important among the ways God's people prepare themselves, however, is to support and encourage one another through participation together in worship and the means of grace and in Christian fellowship.

Vision

During This Week

Urge participants to read and complete at least one of the suggested activities.

Closing Worship

Sing or speak together stanzas 1, 3, and 4 of "Stand Up, Stand Up for Jesus" (*LW* 305) as printed in the Study Guide.

Scripture Lessons for Next Sunday

Assign the appointed lessons for the Third-Last Sunday in the Church Year.

Session 11

Third-Last Sunday in the Church Year

Job 14:1–6; 1 Thessalonians 3:11–13; Matthew 24:15–28

Focus

Theme: *Weeping through the Night, Rejoicing in the Morning*

Law/Gospel Focus

Read aloud the Law/Gospel focus.

Objectives

Invite volunteers to read aloud the lesson objectives.

Opening Worship

Lead the group using the responsive prayer provided.

Introduction

Ask a class member to read aloud the introductory paragraphs. Invite the class to offer general comments or anecdotes to supplement the introduction.

1. Accept all responses. Darkness is often threatening because of our inability to see, the prospect of danger, and our fear of the unknown. The loud noises that accompany storms may disturb children or provoke painful memories in adults.
2. Answers will vary. Some people rely on their own resources and inner strength, while others seek help and cling to family or friends (co-dependent behavior). Some people resort to alcohol or drugs to ease the burdens of the moment. Allow participants to share stories from their experiences, or, where appropriate, of acquaintances.
3. Accept participants' responses.

Inform

If participants have not read the Scripture lessons before class, review the three passages as a class.

1. Job is a wealthy man, with a loving family and large business. Job also is a man of faith. He is tempted by Satan, who according to God's permission and purpose, brings calamity upon Job, his family, and his property. By the end of chapter 2, Job is reduced to extreme poverty and infirmity. Yet He does not curse God or ask to die. His cry of sorrow, then, is prompted by a series of tragic, undeserved hardships.

2. The flower and shadow are perfect illustrations of the transitory nature of human existence. Each of the passages talks about the unavoidable cycle—birth, growth, decay and death—of animal and plant life. The shadow (Ps. 102:11) marks the passage of time and demonstrates the impermanence of life.

3. God opens doors for the ministry of Word and Sacrament to thrive and expand among His people. Paul was seeking an opportunity to visit the congregation at Thessalonica in order to strengthen its faith with his preaching, teaching, and pastoral care. Paul also sought new mission fields, where he could, for the first time, proclaim the Good News of salvation in Christ. God works in history and in ordinary human events to "clear the way" for effective, Gospel-centered ministry.

4. The Holy Spirit works through the Word of life—forgiveness in Jesus—to share the love of Christ in and through God's people. God always desires that His children grow in faith, in righteousness, and in love for all people.

5. Jesus gives His disciples a glimpse of the turmoil and deep human suffering during the last days. False messiahs and prophets will attempt to deceive people, even believers. The picture is one of universal desperation and affliction.

6. God will "cut short" the days of tribulation, that the elect may not be tempted beyond what they are able to endure. See 1 Cor. 10:13. Even in the midst of all types of dangers and opposition, the Lord will guide His people to remain strong in their faith and public confession.

7. Jesus tells the disciples, in essence, to prepare for the cataclysm by focusing upon His Word, drawing strength and comfort from their fellowship together, and by planning, where possible to be ready for the worst.

Connect

Read the introductory section aloud. Emphasize that all throughout Scripture and history, God has been present with His chosen people to rescue them from danger and to guide them to safety. The road from danger to safety is often filled with tremendous hardship. But God is truly waiting to receive us at the end of the struggle.

1. Encourage participants in their responses. Each passage highlights the presence of God and His mighty power to save and provide comfort.
2. The book of James presents Job, who through faith was a model of patience for believers. Job confessed in the face of death, "I know that my Redeemer lives," (Job 19:25), and through all his pain and suffering he kept his eyes on the promise of God—life eternal in Jesus' resurrection. Encourage participants to share an illustration from their lives on patience in the midst of suffering.
3. Answers will vary. For Christians, darkness, in whatever form, will give way to light. The physical, mental and spiritual distress we experience today will, by God's grace, be overcome either some time during this life or eventually in heaven.

Vision

During This Week

Urge participants to read and complete one or more of the suggested activities.

Closing Worship

Sing or speak together stanzas 1–2 and 4 of "Let Us Ever Walk with Jesus" (*LW* 381) as printed in the Study Guide.

Scripture Lessons for Next Sunday

Assign the appointed lessons for the Second-Last Sunday in the Church Year.

Session 12

Second-Last Sunday in the Church Year

Jeremiah 25:30–32; 1 Thessalonians 1:3–10;
Matthew 25:31–46

Focus

Theme: *After the Storm—Grace!*

Law/Gospel Focus

Read aloud the Law/Gospel focus.

Objectives

Invite volunteers to read aloud the lesson objectives.

Opening Worship

Lead the group using the responsive prayer provided.

Introduction

Ask a class member to read aloud the introductory paragraphs. Allow the class to discuss violent weather or natural disasters in your local context, especially in the wake of a recent experience.

1. Encourage participants to share. On an average, 1 of every 10 people have been affected by a serious storm.
2. Answers will vary. Most people, of course, want to be informed in order to make necessary preparations, e.g., purchase supplies, stock up on ice, water, and other ready-to-eat foods. Some people have a fascination with weather patterns, in particular, inclement weather. Many television weather reports actually plot the storm and broadcast the expected time of arrival in different areas. Although no one can alter the course of a storm, there is still a great deal of interest in its path and movement.

3. Accept participants' responses. Non-Christians naturally have no interest in or concern for the Lord's return, but some Christians also show little regard for His second coming. For many, the idea is too remote, or possibly too detached from the demands of everyday life. For others, there may appear to be no reason to prepare: they are confident in their own works or past efforts to earn salvation.

Inform

If participants have not read the Scripture lessons before class, review the three passages as a class.

1. Some of the word pictures are the Lord "thunders," "roars," "shouts," "brings charges," and "punishes." The idea of thunder introduces the storm imagery, and like a loud clap of thunder—a frightening event in ancient times—God speaks a word of judgment or law against the people. "Roar" may allude to the awe-inspiring sound of the lion. "Shout" refers to the cries of celebration while making wine (e.g., joy at the harvest), but in this context it is God's cry of judgment—victory over His enemies. To "tread the winepress" was a figure of judgment. See Joel 3:13 and Rev. 14:17–20. The most obvious picture in the text is the "disaster" and "mighty storm," universal in scope and deadly in effect.

2. The sins of the people are lying, deception, stubbornness, rebellion, unfaithfulness, slander, lovelessness, murder, stealing, adultery, and other grievous acts of defiance before God. God acts as a prosecutor, bringing charges against His people and the nations on the basis of His Word. Note the connection to the Ten Commandments.

3. God's judgment is like a disaster in that it shall come upon the people quickly, without warning, and there is no escape.

4. (a) The Holy Spirit alone works faith in our hearts and minds. God chose us; we do not choose to believe, but God's mercy in Christ brings us to a saving knowledge and trust in Jesus. Faith comes through hearing the Word, the Gospel (Rom. 10:17); faith is powerful, that is, animated and preserved by the power of the Good News (Rom. 1:16–17); faith is always dependent on the Holy Spirit and never or human will or resources; faith is conviction, deep confidence in the truthfulness and faithfulness of God's Word of promise (Heb. 11:1). (b) Answers will vary, but the

knowledge that our sins are forgiven through Christ, and that we stand on the verge of eternity with God, provokes an inner joy that transcends outward circumstances. By the power of the Spirit, we can model our faith for people who need encouragement in their walk with Christ. Allow participants to share personal illustrations. (c) Answers will vary here, too, but one focus might be the assurance of heaven and life forever in the presence of the Lord.

5. Jesus' ministry involved all these acts of care and support:
   - He fed the hungry.
   - He provided living water (John 4:1-42; 7:37–38).
   - He welcomed the strangers, outcasts.
   - He healed the sick.
   - He came to release the prisoners (Luke 4:18–19).

   His disciples are called to carry on His ministry, just as the apostles were sent forth.

   Jesus proclaims His solidarity with the hungry, thirsty, etc., in the words, "whatever you did for one of … these … you did for Me."

6. In the ancient, as today, millions of people suffered from malnutrition and chronic hunger, from thirst (water was often scarce), and from frequent diseases. In addition, because of high mortality rates children and families were often reduced to poverty and to begging from village to village; they were strangers without roots. Purity laws, that is, strict roles of social separation, made certain classes of people outcasts. Prisoners, for political and criminal reasons, faced extreme conditions. But all these problems relate to both physical needs and needs before God: spiritual thirst, hunger (Matt. 5), imprisonment to sin, "soul sickness," etc.

7. Because of the indwelling Holy Spirit, believers desire to serve the Lord through concrete acts of compassion. The parable reminds disciples today that ministry in the name of Jesus is a commitment to the total needs of God's people and the world.

8. The judgment is spoken against those individuals who have no saving faith and thus have no regard for the Lord's call to ministry.

Connect

Read the introductory section aloud.
1. Answers will vary. Jesus' words urge us to follow in His footsteps

and to serve as His instruments of mercy and healing in the world. Ask participants to consider new possibilities for service.

2. Encourage participants to reflect upon their specific situations. Christian love is most often demonstrated in personal, one-on-one acts of kindness.

3. Accept all responses. Allow time for brainstorming as you evaluate opportunities in your community. If a representative of the congregation's social ministry or care ministry is present, invite him or her to describe the program.

Vision

During This Week

Urge participants to read and complete one or more of the suggested activities.

Closing Worship

Sing or speak together "I Love Your Kingdom, Lord" (*LW* 296) as printed in the Study Guide.

Scripture Lessons for Next Sunday

Assign the appointed lessons for the Last Sunday of the Church Year.

Session 13

Last Sunday in the Church Year

Isaiah 65:17–25; 2 Peter 3:3–4, 8–10a, 13; Matthew 25:1–13

Focus

Theme: *Filled with His Fullness*

Law/Gospel Focus

Read aloud the Law/Gospel focus.

Objectives

Invite volunteers to read aloud the lesson objectives.

Opening Worship

Lead the group using the responsive prayer provided.

Introduction

Ask a class member to read aloud the introductory paragraphs. Invite the class to offer anecdotes to supplement the introduction.

1. Accept all responses. Fulfillment is often viewed as acquisition or self-improvement. An individual is content only with a premier position in a firm, a home in an exclusive neighborhood, and a luxury car or two. For others fulfillment may depend on achieving certain goals and pursuing exotic new religions (e.g., New Age movements).

2. Answers will vary. Encourage participants to share honestly. Affirm their experiences where possible, and thank individuals for sharing their stories.

3. Answers will vary. Some participants may point to worship, Bible study, devotional time, fellowship, service organizations, or other facets of congregational life as a tremendous blessing. Also, confidence in Christ enables believers to face the burdens of each day.

Inform

If participants have not already read the Scripture lessons, review the three passages as a class.

1. God promises to forgive and forget our past; there is great joy; sorrow and sickness are banished; believers will dwell securely and permanently in the presence of God; there is a sense of contentment, under God's blessing; God will grant His children's requests; and nothing will harm believers.
2. God no longer remembers our sins, our prideful rebellion, and our faithlessness.
3. The "delay" in the Lord's return caused many pagans in the ancient world to ridicule the idea of a glorious, triumphant return to judge the world. Many scoffed at the idea of divine judgment, as well as the resurrection of the dead. Participant responses may vary on the reasons people scoff today, but may include denial of God's judgment and the hope of resurrection, opposition to supernatural intervention in the world, etc.
4. Answers will vary. For most people "Time, like an ever-rolling stream, Soon bears us all away" ("Our God, Our Help in Ages Past, *Lutheran Worship* 180). Most people, even non-Christians, acknowledge that time passes too quickly. As humans, we become more aware of our limitations, the deterioration of our physical health and strength, and the reality of our death as years go by. God, however, is external. All of the transition and decay we experience is totally outside the realm of God's being and divine purpose. Psalm 90 captures the glory of God's eternal nature and His grandeur and strength.
5. God's patience is shown in His love and compassion, the fact that He is slow to anger and constant in love, and above all, His readiness and willingness to forgive sinners for the sake of Christ. St. Peter expressly identifies the Lord's purpose in delaying judgment: God does not want anyone to perish, but everyone to come to repentance.
6. By his own admission, St. Paul ranks himself as the "worst" sinner of all time. His deeply moving confession applies to every person. All people blaspheme God, go against His will, and even violently break His commandments by their deliberate wickedness and their failure to do good. St. Paul is representative of all humankind. But the "chief of sinners" was shown mercy as a

powerful example of the "unlimited patience" of Jesus Christ (1 Tim. 1:16). This is true comfort to those who feel beyond the scope of God's redemption in Christ. If God called and saved Paul by the Good News, then there is hope for every human being.

7. Allow participants to draw out specific truths and applications from the text. Answers may include anticipation of the event— the wedding feast; the need to plan ahead ("extra oil in jars" is an image granted as a gift from God); a readiness to discern the signs of the master's approach. Encourage discussion.

8. The wise take extra oil; the foolish do not. The wise do not waver in their resolution; the foolish are desperate and uncertain about the situation.

9. Jesus reveals that at the end of time when He returns the time for repentance and faith comes to a close. The cry is urgent: "Now is the time of God's favor, now is the day of salvation" (2 Cor. 6:2). See also Heb. 4:6–7.

Connect

Read the introductory section aloud. Underscore the Word of God as the ultimate authority for what Christians believe, profess, and do. Continue with a discussion of the questions.

1. Encourage participants in their responses. The resurrection is the firstfruits of all who die in faith. Paul notes the sequence: (1) the resurrection of Jesus; (2) the resurrection of the dead, believers to eternal life, unbelievers to eternal condemnation; (3) the close of history and the establishment of the kingdom—God's rule among His people; (4) ultimate destruction of all God's enemies, including death and Satan. In the hymn of Rev. 11:15, 17–18, the angels announce and the elders sing,

"The kingdom of the world has become the kingdom of our Lord and of His Christ,
and He will reign for ever and ever.

… We give thanks to You, Lord God Almighty,
the One who is and who was,
because You have taken Your great power
and have begun to reign.

The nations were angry;
and Your wrath has come.
The time has come for judging the dead,
and for rewarding Your servants the prophets
and Your saints and those who reverence Your name,
both small and great—
and for destroying those who destroy the earth."

2. Answers will vary. We are called to share in His riches, His inheritance, and His mighty power. Christ is now exalted in heaven, but is still present among His people through Word and Sacrament. His body, the church, shares in His fullness on earth and will experience His fullness absolutely in heaven. By the Spirit and through faith, believers know the love of Jesus in its splendor and are filled daily with God's fullness—forgiveness and life.

3. Answers will vary. Allow participants to reflect upon heaven and the Savior's presence.

Vision

During This Week

Urge participants to read and complete one or both of the suggested activities.

Closing Worship

Sing or speak together "Wake, Awake, for Night Is Flying" (*LW* 177) as printed in the Study Guide.

Scripture Lessons for the Reformation

Assign the appointed lessons for the Reformation.

Session 14

Reformation

Jeremiah 31:31–34; Romans 3:19–28; John 8:31–36

===== **Focus** =====

Theme: *Free in Christ Indeed!*

Law/Gospel Focus

Read aloud the Law/Gospel focus.

Objectives

Invite volunteers to read aloud the lesson objectives.

Opening Worship

Lead the group using the responsive prayer provided.

Introduction

Invite a class member to read aloud the introductory paragraphs.
1. Accept all responses offered. The "chains" of modern life may include financial and employment obligations, the frantic pace of family and social commitments, the desire or "need" to be avid consumers in order to "get ahead" or "keep up," or other personal problems and compulsions. All these "masters" can dictate people's schedules and dominate their priorities, so that in fact they become slaves, working for the means rather than toward the goal (presumably, that is, a happy, healthy, and balanced life).
2. Some people think freedom is the ability to do whatever they want: absolute independence from any responsibility or restraint. Others view freedom as having a certain latitude to move around within the rules; that is, people can make basic choices, but they must stay within the recognized boundaries. On the American scene, there are individuals who equate freedom with the right to engage in destructive and dangerous behavior, even at the expense of another's personal safety. All of these are distorted

notions of freedom. Allow the class to offer current illustrations of the abuse of freedom.

3. Accept participants' responses. Webster's Collegiate Dictionary (10th edition) offers the following definitions for freedom: "the absence of necessity, coercion, or constraint in choice or action;" "liberation from slavery or restraint or from the power of another;" "the quality or state of being exempt or released from something onerous." Yet real freedom, as God intends, includes both being delivered, that is, liberated, from something and responsible to something. So often the world neglects the idea of freedom for, or responsibility toward, what is good and beneficial for the whole, not simply the part. Share with the participants the famous saying of Luther on Christian liberty: "A Christian is a free lord of all and subject to no one. A Christian is a ministering servant of all and subject to everyone" (*What Luther Says*). His insight provides an excellent starting point for the discussion of freedom, both in its secular context and in reference to Christian faith and discipleship.

Inform

If participants have not read the Scripture lessons before class, review the three passages as a class.

1. As you examine the covenants God made with His people, keep in mind that God is both the source and the strength of the relationship. A helpful chart of "Major Covenants in the Old Testament" is listed in the *Concordia Self-Study Bible*, page 18.

Noah: God's covenant with Noah was, "never again will there be a flood to destroy the earth" (Gen. 9:11). God has kept His promise, and even in the end will not consume humankind and creation by water.

Abraham: God's covenant is to bless Abraham and to make his descendants into a mighty family. From Abraham, God declares, a child of promise will come, a promise which finds fulfillment in the birth of the Messiah, Jesus. St. Paul writes, "Understand, then, that those who believe are children of Abraham. The Scripture foresaw that God would justify the Gentiles by faith, and announced the gospel in advance to Abraham: 'All nations will be blessed through you.' So those who have faith are blessed along with Abraham, the man of faith" (Gal. 3:7–9). The promise to the seed, or offspring (Gen. 12:7), refers to Christ: The promises were spoken to Abraham and to his seed. "The Scripture does not say 'and to seeds,' meaning many people, but 'and to your seed,' meaning one person, who is Christ" (Gal. 3:16).

Sinai: The covenant with Israel is rooted in God's rescue of His people from captivity in Egypt. He promised to redeem them from slavery for a life of faith, service and holiness, and He kept His promise.

David: God promised to build David a "house," that is, a dynasty, from which the Messiah would come, the King and Shepherd of God's chosen people. The Father fulfilled His Word in the birth of His Son, the "Savior ... Christ the Lord" (Luke 2:11).

2. God promises to put His law in the minds and on the hearts of His people, and to grant an intimate knowledge of His Word and will. For the Israelites, this was primarily a matter of divine forgiveness and restoration. In the light of their sinful past, a fresh start, a new relationship with God, was a spark of light and joy in the midst of all their recent hardships (the destruction of Jerusalem and their exile in Babylon). The promise was meaningful because God would bring it to pass, not as a result of the people's initiative or effort, but because of His steadfast love and mercy.

3. To "know the Lord" is a common biblical phrase for faith and a saving understanding of God and His Word through both Law and Gospel. Knowledge of God is dependent upon revelation, first of all in creation, but primarily in and through His Word. Moses was privileged to see the glory of God that he might lead God's people forward in their mission. The passages in the Study Guide highlight different facets of knowing God and what knowledge of God entails in the lives of God's people. Knowledge is a gift of the Spirit, and focuses upon Christ, His death and resurrection for the salvation of the world, and an intimate awareness of the Savior's Word to His disciples.

4. Answers will vary, but will likely include offering to God the following statements: (1) I tried my best. (2) I did everything you asked. (3) I'm not as bad as some other people. (4) Here's all I accomplished in life. (5) I kept all the Commandments, never killed anyone, stole anything, etc. Paul announces, "No one will be declared righteous in [God's] sight by observing the law" (Rom. 3:20).

5. The list can include sinners, disobedient, hostile to God, alienated, separated, enemies, faithless, etc.

6. The list can include justified, forgiven, redeemed, reconciled, saved, delivered, rescued, blessed, etc.

7. Believers "hold" to the Lord's teaching by first of all hearing and trusting His Word, by learning it and applying it to our lives, by continuing to study and meditate upon it, and by putting it into practice every day (obedience). Jesus says "Remain in Me, and I will remain in you. … [You] will bear much fruit" (John 15:4, 5). The person who does not remain in Jesus is like a branch ready to be thrown away (John 15:6). "If you remain in Me and My words remain in you, ask whatever you wish …" (John 15:7).

   "Remain in My love. If you obey My commands, you will remain in My love …" (John 15:9–10).

   The word *hold* in John 8:31 is the same word translated as "remain" in John 15. The idea, at root, is to continue in, to remain connected to and dependent upon, what one has received.

8. The disciples deny ever being in slavery, but in fact the people of God had been enslaved by different nations at various times in history (Egypt, Assyria, and Babylonia). During Jesus' ministry, the people of Judea and Jerusalem were largely under Roman occupation, and virtual slaves of Rome. Their words betray their deception and enslavement: they are under the command of Satan, the liar and father of lies (John 8:44).

9. Allow participants to share their perceptions and experience. Certain sins, such as sexual immorality, greed, and addiction seem to entice people into a prison from which they cannot escape. St. Paul in Romans 7 presents his own and the universal human experience of life under sin and the weight of the Law.

10. A child of God may call upon God as Father at all times and in all places and rely upon Him to answer prayers.

Connect

Read the introductory section aloud. Underscore the Word of God as the ultimate authority for what Christians believe, profess, and do. Continue with a discussion of the questions.

1. Encourage participants to look up the passages listed in the Study Guide and to write down the blessings of freedom in Christ. We are, for example, free from the power of sin, death, and the devil, from anxiety and fear and the burden of self-justification. We are free to serve the Lord and His people, to live

responsibly as Christian citizens in our nation, free to move forward in our mission, and free to live in Christ's forgiveness, although we daily sin against His Word.

2. Paul exhorts the congregation to "stand firm" in Christ's freedom, purchased by His death on the cross. The issues are that the Galatians have turned to "a different gospel" (Gal. 1:6), a false gospel that insists upon human works for full justification before God. Some members of the congregation wanted to make the keeping of the Law an essential part of salvation. All of these, however, bring us back to slavery. Christ's death alone frees us from the Law and from sin. To return to the Law is to be "burdened again by a yoke of slavery" (Gal. 5:1).

   On the other hand, Paul admonishes the congregation to understand their freedom in Christ as a costly gift from God. Indulging the sinful nature demonstrates contempt for the Lord's sacrifice for our forgiveness. The principle is often stated in Paul's writings: "You are not your own; you were bought at a price. Therefore honor God with your body" (1 Cor. 6:19–20; 7:23).

3. Allow participants to respond. St. Paul boasts only about Christ's forgiveness and love in his life, and nothing else!

4. Answers will vary, but the Reformation doctrine of "justification by grace, for Christ's sake, through faith" (Augsburg Confession, article 4), seeks to ascribe all glory to the Trinity for our creation, redemption, and sanctification. *Soli Deo gloria:* To God alone be the glory!

Vision

During This Week

Urge participants to read and complete one or more of the suggested activities.

Closing Worship

Sing or speak together stanzas 1, 2, and 5 of "By Grace I'm Saved" (*LW* 351) as printed in the Study Guide.

Scripture Lessons for All Saints' Day

Assign the appointed lessons for All Saints' Day.

Session 15

All Saints' Day

Isaiah 26:1–4, 8–9, 12–13, 19–21; Revelation 21:9–11,
22–27, (22:1–5); Matthew 5–12

Focus

Theme: *The Blessed Event*

Law/Gospel Focus
Read aloud the Law/Gospel focus.

Objectives
Invite volunteers to read aloud the lesson objectives.

Opening Worship
Lead the group using the responsive prayer provided.

Introduction

Ask a class member to read aloud the introductory paragraphs.
Invite the class to offer anecdotes to supplement the introduction.
 1. Responses will vary. Each of the statements conveys an important
    truth from the perspective of salvation in Christ. No statement is
    complete in itself or tells the entire story, but together provide a
    foundation for the Christian understanding of death. Allow par-
    ticipants to reflect their unique perspectives.
 2. Answers will vary.
 3. Allow participants to respond as time permits.

Inform

If participants have not read the Scripture lessons before class,
review the three passages as a class.
 1. The glory of heaven is the glory of God's absolute power and gra-
    cious design for His creation. A fortified city in the ancient world
    was a haven in the midst of war, attacks from bandits, and other
    man-made and natural disasters. The inhabitants of a well-

stocked, well-defended city could dwell in safety, in spite of the tribulation all around, outside the walls. A fortified city radiated a sense of permanence and stability, like a great mountain. Like the city of His building, God is also a mighty fortress, a rock eternal.

2. God makes the city and its walls strong; He maintains His people and establishes peace in their midst; He accomplishes everything the people now enjoy; He will come to raise His people from the dust of death and to judge the world in righteousness.

3. God summons His people to death: "Go … enter your rooms and shut the doors" is an apt image for burial and bodily rest in the time before the general resurrection. At the day of judgment, when God comes from heaven to punish all human wickedness and save His chosen people, the doors will be opened and the dead will be raised to condemnation or to life eternal with Christ. Luther's comments are relevant to the passage.

> You must not judge … by external appearances; you must be guided by the Word, which promises and gives you everlasting life. … But you will retort: "The fact remains that I must die." Oh, this makes no difference! Just go ahead and die in God's name, … You are still assured of eternal life; it will surely be yours. To die, to be buried, to have people tread on your grave … all this will not matter to you. It is certain that Christ will raise you up again. *(Luther's Works)*

4. The relationship of Christ to the church is closer and more perfect than the best human marriage relationship. Earlier in the chapter (21:2), the church is compared to a bride, beautifully dressed for the wedding. St. Paul extends the marriage analogy to describe the intimacy and union between the Lord and the church; "Christ loved the church and gave Himself up for her to make her holy, cleansing her by the washing with water through the word, and to present her to Himself as a radiant church, without stain or wrinkle or any other blemish, but holy and blameless" (Eph. 5:26–27). The relationship of husband and wife is a mirror—often imperfect—of an even deeper mystery: "I am talking about Christ and the church," St. Paul notes (Eph. 5:32).

5. The light of God and the Lamb signify the perpetual glory of the Triune God, the fact that God will forever be with His chosen and redeemed people. The city gates are never closed because there is never the danger of attack or disaster; God is the protector and the provider of all good gifts.

6. A person's name is written in the Book of Life through the blood of the Lamb. The fact that Christ has written our names into eternity by His death and resurrection brings great comfort, for there is no reason to strive after salvation through our own energy and endeavors.

7. Blessedness, according to Luther, is being "blessed before God and by God." A believer can certainly feel, accept as true, and experience blessedness. Blessedness is both the pronouncement and the gift of grace that enables a disciple of the Lord Jesus to live in His forgiveness and to approach all of life, as well as to endure all life's challenges and obstacles, with His strength alone. Blessedness is, of course, God's gift, as the Holy Spirit works through the Word to keep God's people in His grace.

Listen to Luther on the Beatitudes.

> What a dear and wonderful Preacher and faithful Master! He leaves out nothing that will help to strengthen and console, whether it be His Word and promise or the example and testimony of all the saints and of Himself. And all the angels in heaven and all the creatures support this. What more would you want and need? (*Luther's Works*)

8. Answers will vary. Allow participants to draw upon their experiences, or to reflect upon opportunities for spiritual growth.

9. The Beatitudes are the Lord's words of grace and Good News for His disciples—not rules or suggestions, but a pattern for following His ways and living under His gentle yoke (Matt. 11:28–30). Our discipleship on earth is, and will be as long as we live, imperfect. In the eternal kingdom, heaven, Jesus' call to follow will be fulfilled, as His presence will guide and bless us always.

Connect

Read the introductory section aloud. You may wish to refer to the hymnal or catechism for the Third Article of the Apostles' Creed and its explanation.

1. Ask for volunteers to share a brief story of the joy of Christian faith and fellowship. Affirm all the participants who relate their experiences.

2. God has prepared a royal "homecoming" for His children. Jesus speaks to the disciples, "In my Father's house are many rooms; if

it were not so, I would have told you. I am going there to prepare a place for you. And if I go and prepare a place for you, I will come back and take you to be with Me that you also may be where I am" (John 14:2–3). The Lord promises to escort us through death to heaven, because He is "the way and the truth and the life" (John 14:6).

3. Allow any or all participants to describe their funeral plans or wishes. Although this may seem like a somber exercise for the class, use the occasion to emphasize the hope and comfort we have in Christ as we contemplate death.

Vision

During This Week

Urge participants to read and complete one or both of the suggested activities during the coming week.

Closing Worship

Sing or speak together stanzas 1, 2, 4 and 8 of "For All the Saints" (*LW* 191) as printed in the Study Guide.

Scripture Lessons for Next Sunday

Assign the appointed lessons for first Sunday in Advent.